CANON
EOS R7
POCKET GUIDE

TABLE OF CONTENTS

04 OTHER HELPFUL SETTINGS

05 STEP-BY-STEP SHOOTING INSTRUCTIONS

06 TYPICAL SHOOTING SCENARIOS

01 PRE-SHOOT CHECKLIST

Check these settings before you head out with your camera!

SETTING	MY PREFERRED SETTING
☑ Shooting Mode	....
☑ White Balance Setting	....
☑ ISO Setting	....
☑ Exposure Compensation	....
☑ Focus Mode	....
☑ Focus Method	....
☑ Drive Mode	....
☑ Metering Mode	....
☑ Picture Style	....
☑ Bracketing Setting	....
☑ Highlight Alert Setting	....
☑ File Format: RAW, JPEG, or RAW & JPEG	....
☑ Battery Fully Charged and in Camera	....
☑ Memory Card(s) Formatted and in Camera	....

02 BUTTONS, DIALS, AND SCREENS

CAMERA TOP

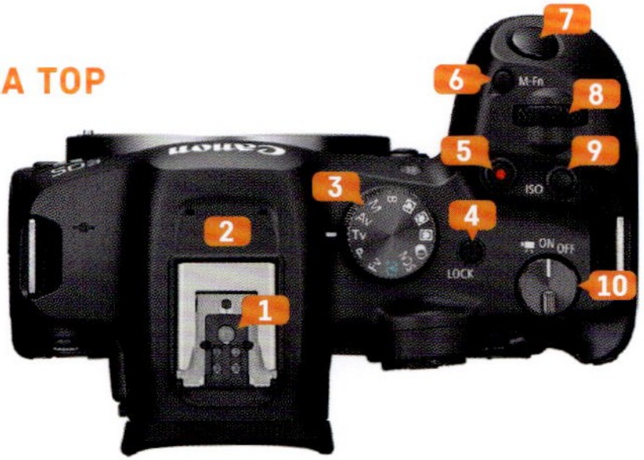

1. **Multi-Function Shoe:** Used for external flash or other accessories.
2. **Microphone:** Built-in stereo microphones.
3. **Mode Dial:** Use this dial to set the shooting mode.
4. **LOCK (Multi-Function Lock) Button:** Prevents settings from being changed if you accidentally operate the Main Dial, Quick Control Dial, or the lens's Control Ring.
5. **Movie Shooting Button:** Press to start and stop recording a movie.
6. **Multi-Function (M-Fn) Button:** Press this button in combination with turning the Quick Control Dial to set the drive mode, AF (autofocus) operation, white balance, and flash exposure compensation.
7. **Shutter Button:** Press halfway to activate autofocus; press all the way to take a photo.
8. **Main Dial:** Use this dial to set the shutter speed, aperture, and other settings.
9. **ISO Button:** Use to set the ISO.
10. **Video/On/Off Switch:** Turns the camera on and off, or changes to video mode.

CAMERA FRONT

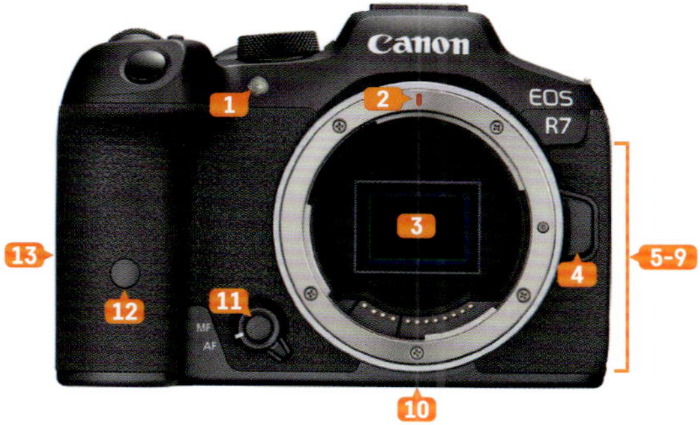

1. **AF-Assist Beam/Self-Timer:** Lights up area in front of camera in low light. Blinks when Self-Timer is active.
2. **Lens Mounting Mark:** Use to line up lens and camera when mounting a lens.
3. **Image Sensor:** The 32.5-megapixel APS-C sensor.
4. **Lens Release Button:** Press to remove lens.
5. **Microphone Terminal:** Connect external microphone to camera (under cover).
6. **HDMI Out Terminal:** Connect HDMI micro cable (under cover).
7. **Remote Terminal:** Connect wired remote to camera (under cover).
8. **Digital Terminal:** Connect to digital devices (under cover).
9. **Headphone Terminal:** Connect headphone to camera (under cover).
10. **Tripod Socket:** Standard threaded tripod socket (bottom of camera).
11. **Focus Mode Switch:** Switches between autofocus and manual focus.
12. **Remote Control Sensor:** Used with a wireless camera remote.
13. **Memory Card Compartment:** Open to access memory cards (side of camera).

CAMERA BACK

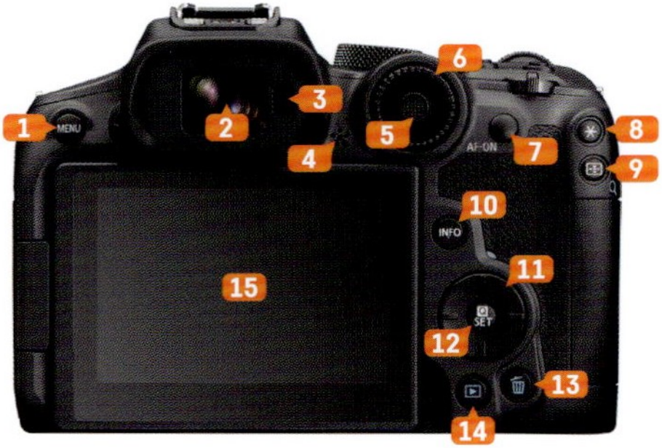

1. **MENU Button:** Press to bring up Menu options.
2. **Diopter Adjustment:** Use this to adjust the viewfinder display focus for your eye.
3. **Viewfinder Sensor:** Senses when you're looking through the viewfinder and activates the viewfinder display.
4. **Speaker:** Built-in speaker.
5. **Multi-Controller:** Use this for operations such as white balance correction, autofocus (AF) point movement, magnifying the frame during playback, Quick Control setting adjustments, etc. Can also be used to select or set menu items.
6. **Quick Control Dial:** Use this dial to set exposure compensation, aperture while in Manual shooting mode, etc.
7. **AF Start (AF-ON) Button:** Press to engage the autofocus.
8. **AE Lock Button:** Use to lock exposure.
9. **AF Point Selection Button:** Use to select the desired autofocus (AF) point.

10. INFO Button: Press to cycle through views displaying different information.

11. Quick Control (Q)/SET Button: Use to access the Quick Control screen. Use SET to finalize a setting and return to a previous screen.

12. Cross Keys: The cross keys can be used to navigate menus and selections. Trash erases the current photo on display.

13. Trash Button: Trash erases the current photo on display.

14. Playback Button: Press to view the last image taken.

15. Screen: Displays multiple features, options, and settings for shooting and playback. Touch screen can be used to quickly adjust camera settings.

STILL SHOOTING SCREEN

Each time you press the INFO button, the information display will change. The display will show only the settings currently applied.

Note: Viewfinder display positions will vary for some items.

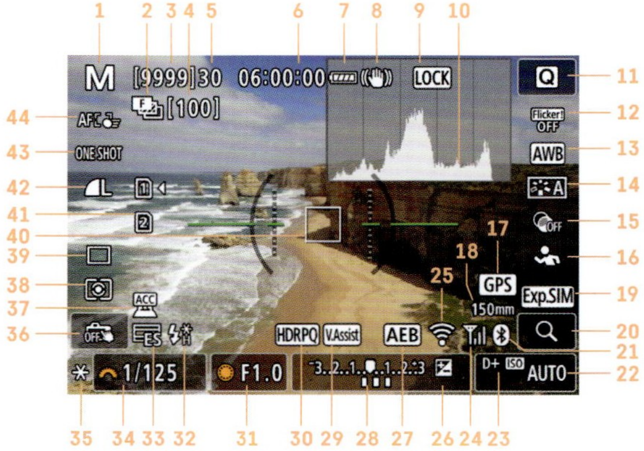

1. **Shooting Mode**
2. **Focus Bracketing/HDR/Multiple Exposures/Multi Shot Noise Reduction/Bulb Timer/Interval Timer**
3. **Number of Available Shots/Seconds Until Self-Timer Shoots**
4. **Number of Remaining Shots for Focus Bracketing, Multiple Exposures, or Interval Timer**
5. **Maximum Burst**
6. **Movie Recording Time Available**
7. **Battery Level**
8. **Image Stabilization (IS Mode)**

9. Multi-Function Lock Warning
10. Histogram
11. Quick Control Button
12. Anti-Flicker Shooting
13. White Balance/White Balance Correction
14. Picture Style
15. Creative Filters
16. Subject to Detect
17. GPS
18. Focal Length
19. Exposure Simulation
20. Magnify Button
21. Bluetooth Function
22. ISO Speed
23. Highlight Tone Priority
24. Wi-Fi Signal Strength
25. Wi-Fi Function
26. Exposure Compensation
27. AEB/FEB (Auto Exposure Bracketing/Flash Exposure Bracketing)
28. Exposure Level Indicator
29. View Assist
30. HDR PQ
31. Aperture Value
32. Flash Ready/FE (Flash Exposure) Lock/High-Speed Sync
33. Electronic Shutter
34. Shutter Speed
35. AE (Auto Exposure) Lock
36. Touch Shutter/Create Folder
37. Accessory Attached Indicator
38. Metering Mode
39. Drive Mode
40. AF Point (1-Point AF)
41. Memory Cards
42. Image Quality
43. AF Operation
44. AF Area

MOVIE SHOOTING SCREEN

Each time you press the INFO button, the information display will change. The display will show only the settings currently applied.

Note: Viewfinder display positions will vary for some items.

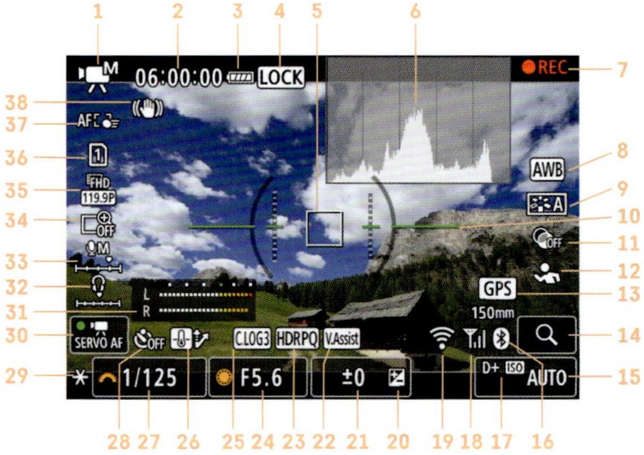

1. **Movie Shooting Mode**
2. **Movie Recording Time Available/Elapsed Recording Time**
3. **Battery Level**
4. **Multi-Function Lock Warning**
5. **AF Point (1-Point AF)**
6. **Histogram (Brightness/RGB)**
7. **Recording in Progress**

8. White Balance/White Balance Correction
9. Picture Style
10. Electronic Level
11. Creative Filters
12. Subject to Track
13. GPS
14. Magnify Button
15. ISO Speed
16. Highlight Tone Priority
17. Bluetooth Function
18. Wi-Fi Signal Strength
19. Wi-Fi Function
20. Exposure Compensation
21. Exposure Level Indicator (Metering Levels)
22. View Assist
23. HDR PQ
24. Aperture Value
25. Canon Log
26. Overheat Control
27. Shutter Speed
28. Movie Self-Timer
29. AE (Auto Exposure) Lock
30. Movie Servo AF
31. Audio Recording Level Indicator (Manual)
32. Headphone Volume
33. Audio Recording Level
34. Digital Zoom
35. Movie Recording Size
36. Card Used for Movie Recording
37. AF Area
38. Image Stabilization

03 ESSENTIAL MODES AND SETTINGS

SHOOTING MODES

Rotate the Mode dial to the desired shooting mode.

A+ (Scene Intelligent Auto): The camera assesses the scene and sets the optimum settings automatically. It will even adjust the focus on both still and moving subjects.

SCN: These Special Scene modes use the appropriate settings for the type of scene you select. Press the SET button, turn the Main dial to select a special scene mode, then press the SET button again. Choose from Portrait, Group Photo, Landscape, Panoramic Shot, Sports, Kids, Panning, Close-Up, Food, Night Portrait, Handheld Night Scene, HDR Backlight Control, and Silent Shutter.

Creative Filter Mode: These special effects can be applied before the photo is taken, allowing you to preview the effect. Press the SET button, turn the Main dial to select a filter effect, then press SET again. Choose from Grainy B/W, Soft Focus, Fish-Eye, Water Painting, Toy Camera, Miniature, HDR Art Standard, HDR Art Vivid, HDR Art Bold, and HDR Art Embossed.

Fv (Flexible-Priority AE): Shutter speed, aperture, and ISO are all set automatically, then you can change one, two, or all three settings to get the desired exposure. The settings you don't change will automatically be adjusted by the camera.

P (Program AE): The camera sets the shutter speed and aperture based on metering info and current ISO.

Tv (Time Value, or Shutter Speed Priority): You set the shutter speed and the camera sets the aperture based on metering info and current ISO.

Av (Aperture Value, or Aperture Priority): You set the aperture, and the camera sets the shutter speed based on metering info and current ISO. Range of available apertures depends on the attached lens.

M (Manual): You set ISO, shutter speed, and aperture. Refer to the exposure level indicator.

B (Bulb – Long Exposures): Used for long exposures, the shutter stays open as long as you hold down the shutter button. Use the Main dial to set the aperture.

C1, C2, C3 (Custom Shooting Modes): Use the Set-Up Menu to set a custom shooting mode.

METERING MODES

Menu > Shooting (Screen 3) > Metering Mode

Evaluative: General-purpose mode suited for most situations and subjects (even backlit subjects).

Partial: Uses medium-sized area at the center of the screen for determining exposure. Good choice when there is very bright light around the subject.

Spot: Uses small area at the center of the screen. Use when you need to meter on a specific part of the scene.

Center-Weighted Average: The camera analyzes the whole scene to determine exposure, but places more emphasis on info at the center of the screen.

EXPOSURE COMPENSATION

Press Shutter button halfway down, then rotate the Quick Control Dial to adjust exposure compensation, from −3 (darker) to +3 (lighter) stops, in 1/3-stop increments.

When shooting in the Fv Shooting mode, set the shutter speed, aperture, and ISO. Turn the Quick Control Dial to select an item to set, then use the Main dial to set the option.

To reset the exposure compensation back to 0, press the Erase/Trash button.

FOCUS OPERATION

MENU > AF (Screen 1) > AF Operation

One Shot AF: Focus starts when Shutter button is pressed halfway, then locks when focus is achieved. Best for stationary subjects.

Servo: Focus starts when Shutter button is pressed halfway and continues to focus until photo is taken. Best for moving subjects.

Note: For **Manual focus**, set the AF/MF switch on the lens to MF, and rotate the focus ring on the lens barrel to focus.

AUTOFOCUS AREA

MENU > AF (Screen 1) > AF Area

Spot AF: The camera focuses on the smallest possible area, even narrower than 1-Point AF.

1-Point AF: The camera focuses using a single point for critical focus.

Expand AF Area: The camera uses one AF point, as well as the points adjacent and nearby to that focus point to help focus. Helpful for moving subjects that are difficult to track with 1-Point AF.

Expand AF Area: Around: The camera creates an even larger area around one AF point to find focus.

Flexible Zone AF 1: The camera automatically picks focus point using a large square area. Generally will focus on the nearest subject.

Flexible Zone AF 2: The camera automatically picks focus point using a vertical rectangular area. Generally will focus on the nearest subject.

Flexible Zone AF 3: The camera automatically picks focus point using a horizontal rectangular area. Generally will focus on the nearest subject.

Whole Area AF: Uses the whole area to pick the focus point, based on nearest subject, faces present, subject motion, subject distance, and more.

AUTOFOCUS TRACKING

Use the following menu options to set autofocus tracking:

MENU > AF (Screen 1) > Subject Tracking: Turns subject tracking on or off.

MENU > AF (Screen 1) > Subject to Detect: Choose from People, Animals, Vehicles, or None.

MENU > AF (Screen 1) > Eye Detection: Works to get the eyes of people or animals in focus.

MENU > AF (Screen 1) > Switching Tracked Subjects: Changes how quickly the camera switches from one subject to another.

ADDITIONAL AUTOFOCUS OPTIONS

Move the AF Point or Zone AF Frame: Use the Multi-Controller to move the point to the desired location. To center the AF point, press the Multi-Controller straight in. You can also tap directly on the screen to select the focus point.

Magnified View: To check focus, you can magnify the view approximately 5x or 10x by tapping the Magnify button. Magnification is centered on the currently selected AF point. Pressing the Shutter button halfway down will activate the autofocus in magnified view.

Preview AF: MENU > AF (Screen 3) > Preview AF. When enabled, the camera keeps the subject generally in focus, which reduces the focusing time needed when you press the Shutter button halfway down. This does deplete the battery faster.

Manual Focus Peaking: MENU > AF (Screen 5) > MF Peaking Settings. When manually focusing, focus peaking informs you that focus has been achieved by lighting up when edges of subject are in focus.

DRIVE MODES

Press the M-Fn (Multi-Function) button and rotate the Quick Control Dial to select Drive Mode option, then rotate Main dial to select the desired mode.

Single Shooting: The camera takes a single shot every time Shutter button is fully pressed.

High-Speed Continuous Shooting +: The camera takes up to 15 frames per second when you press and hold the Shutter button (or 30 frames per second in Electronic Shutter mode).

High-Speed Continuous Shooting: The camera takes up to 6.5 frames per second in Mechanical Shutter mode, 8 frames per second in Electronic 1st-curtain Shutter mode, and 15 frames per second in Electronic Shutter mode, when you press and hold the Shutter button.

Low-Speed Continuous Shooting: The camera takes up to 3 frames per second when you press and hold the Shutter button.

Self-Timer 10: Sets the self-timer for 10 seconds.

Self-Timer 2: Sets the self-timer for 2 seconds.

Self-Timer Continuous: Shoot 2–10 photos every 10 seconds.

SHUTTER MODE

MENU > Shooting (Screen 7) > Shutter Mode

Mechanical: Uses the mechanical shutter. Recommended when shooting wide open with fast glass.

Electronic 1st-curtain: The front curtain opens silently; taking the photos uses the mechanical rear curtain.

Electronic: This uses the electronic curtain for the whole photograph with no shutter noise. Image quality may be impacted.

WHITE BALANCE

Press the M-Fn (Multi-Function) button and rotate the Quick Control Dial to select the White Balance option, then rotate Main dial to select the desired setting.

Auto (AWB) (Ambience Priority) setting is best for most situations. **AWB-W** (White Priority) is best when you want to reduce a warm color cast. White balance can be set to shift colors warmer, cooler, or keep them accurate. Other settings are all matched to different lighting types. For truest colors, pick the type of lighting being used to illuminate the scene.

FILE FORMATS

MENU > Shooting (Screen 1) > Image Quality. Use the Main dial to select the RAW quality, and use the Quick Control Dial to select the JPEG/HEIF quality. Press the SET button to apply it.

RAW/C-RAW (Compact RAW): The RAW data from the image sensor is recorded each time a photo is taken. The C-RAW version is a compressed RAW file that takes up less space.

RAW/JPEG: If you have selected both a RAW and JPEG option, the camera saves two files each time the Shutter button is pressed: a RAW file and a JPEG file. You also decide the size of the JPEG (fine, normal, large, medium, small).

JPEG: The camera saves a JPEG file each time the Shutter button is pressed. You also decide the size of the JPEG.

HEIF: This file type is used for HDR photography and can be converted to JPEG after shooting.

Dual Pixel RAW: Menu > Shooting (Screen 1) > Dual Pixel Raw. Record RAW or C-RAW images containing dual pixel information from the sensor. This allows you to fine-tune the apparent resolution using depth information, shift the camera viewpoint slightly, and reduce ghosting when using Canon EOS Digital Photo Professional software. Result can vary depending on the situation.

04 OTHER HELPFUL SETTINGS

DISPLAY SIMULATION

MENU > Shooting (Screen 9) > Display Simulation.

This feature displays a simulation of the current exposure settings (image brightness) and depth of field.

Exposure + DOF: The displayed image brightness and depth of field will more closely match the actual exposure and depth of field of the final photo.

Exposure: The image brightness that is displayed will more closely match the actual brightness of your shots.

Exposure Only During DOF: Exposure Simulation is turned off unless you press and hold the depth-of-field preview button, in which case you will see the exposure simulation and the depth-of-field preview.

Disable (OFF): The image will be shown with the standard brightness.

PICTURE STYLES

MENU > Shooting (Screen 4) > Picture Style

Allows you to adjust settings for JPEG images. Adjustable settings are Sharpness (Strength, Fineness, Threshold), Contrast, Saturation, Color Tone, Filter Effect (Monochrome), and Toning Effect (Monochrome). Eight preset picture controls can all be adjusted: **A (Auto), S (Standard), P (Portrait), L (Landscape), FD (Fine Detail), N (Neutral), F (Faithful), M (Monochrome)**. The Monochrome also has four color filters—Yellow, Orange, Red, and Green, or None—and four toning effects—Sepia, Blue, Purple, and Green, or None. Finally, there are also three User-Defined Picture Styles, which allow you to customize any of the styles for easy access.

CUSTOM WHITE BALANCE

Setting a custom White Balance can help you get the best color when you're shooting under mixed lighting:

1. Take a photo of a white card (or white wall) under the mixed lighting at the scene. Be sure to fill the screen (this may require you to switch to manual focus to create the exposure).
2. Select MENU > Shooting (Screen 4) > Custom White Balance.

04 OTHER HELPFUL SETTINGS

05 STEP-BY-STEP SHOOTING INSTRUCTIONS

06 TYPICAL SHOOTING SCENARIOS

01 PRE-SHOOT CHECKLIST

Check these settings before you head out with your camera!

SETTING	MY PREFERRED SETTING
☑ Shooting Mode	....
☑ White Balance Setting	....
☑ ISO Setting	....
☑ Exposure Compensation	....
☑ Focus Operation	....
☑ Focus Area	....
☑ Drive Mode	....
☑ Metering Mode	....
☑ Picture Style	....
☑ Bracketing Setting	....
☑ Highlight Alert Setting	....
☑ Highlight Tone Priority Setting	....
☑ File Format: RAW, JPEG, or RAW & JPEG	....
☑ Battery Fully Charged and In Camera	....
☑ Memory Cards Formatted and In Camera	....

02 BUTTONS, DIALS, AND SCREENS

CAMERA BODY TOP

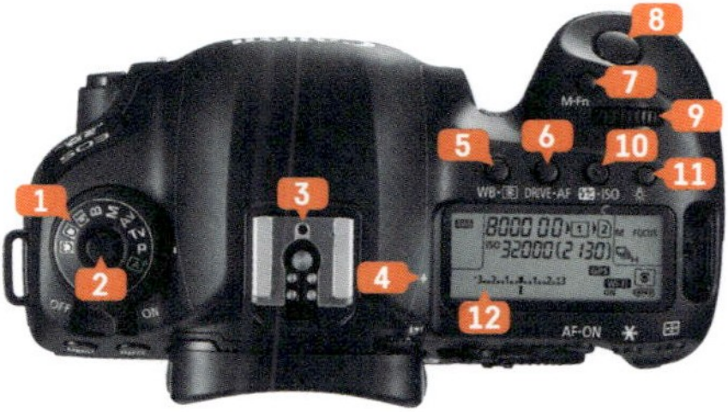

1. **Mode Dial:** Turn to set the shooting mode.
2. **Mode Dial Lock-Release Button:** Press and hold to unlock the Mode Dial.
3. **Hot Shoe:** Use to mount an external flash or other accessory that uses the camera's hot shoe.
4. **Focal Plane Mark:** Use to measure the exact distance to the focal plane of the camera's sensor.
5. **White Balance/Metering Mode Button:** Press this button, then rotate the Quick Command Dial to change the white balance/Press this button, then rotate the Main Dial to change the metering mode.

6. **Drive Mode/Autofocus (AF) Operation Button:** Press and hold this button while rotating the Quick Command Dial to change the drive mode/Press and release this button, then rotate the Main Command Dial to change the autofocus operation.

7. **Multi-Function (M-Fn) Button:** By default, this is set to change the AF Area mode, but it can be customized in the Custom Functions (Screen 3) > Custom Controls menu.

8. **Shutter Release Button:** Press halfway down to lock exposure and autofocus, and press all the way down to take the photo.

9. **Main Dial:** Use to select or change settings on the camera.

10. **Flash Compensation/ISO Button:** Press this button, then rotate the Quick Command Dial to change the flash compensation/Press this button, then rotate Main Command Dial to change the ISO.

11. **LCD Panel Illumination Button:** Press to illuminate the LCD panel.

12. **LCD Panel:** Shows setting information. Details in "LCD Panel" section below.

CAMERA BODY BACK

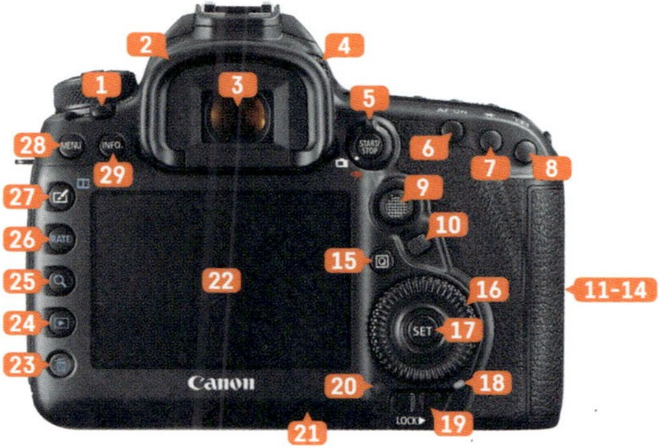

1. **Power Switch:** Turns the camera on and off.
2. **Eyecup:** Soft rubber piece that blocks light from entering the viewfinder when your eye is pressed against it.
3. **Viewfinder:** Shows the view through the attached lens.
4. **Diopter Adjustment:** Used to correct the viewfinder view for your eyesight.
5. **Live View and Movie Switch/Start-Stop Button:** Switch between Live View and Movie shooting modes, then press the button to start the selected mode and press again to stop and return to viewfinder photography.
6. **AF-On Button:** Press this to start autofocus instead of pressing halfway down on the Shutter Release button.
7. **AE Lock Button:** When this button is pressed, the exposure settings become locked, allowing you to recompose the scene without the exposure changing. Press a second time to unlock the exposure settings.

8. AF Point Selection Button: Allows you to select the autofocus point you want to use.

9. Multi-Controller: A joystick-style controller used for selecting and setting menu items, selecting the autofocus point, scrolling around a magnified image on the LCD, and adjusting the white balance.

10. AF-Area Selection Button: By default, this is set the same as the M-Fn button. Press the AF Point Selection button, then this button to cycle through the available AF area modes. You can also customize this button in the Custom Functions (Screen 3) > Custom Controls menu.

11. Card Slot Cover: The memory card slots are under the cover.

12. SD Card Slot (Under Cover): Where the SD card is inserted.

13. CF Card Slot (Under Cover): Where the Compact Flash card is inserted.

14. CF Card Eject Button (Under Cover): Press to eject the Compact Flash card.

15. Quick Control Button: Press to open the Quick Control screen.

16. Quick Control Dial: Use to navigate through menus or select shooting options.

17. SET Button: Selects a highlighted menu item or setting.

18. Access Lamp: The light illuminates or blinks when the memory card is being accessed. Do not turn the camera off or eject the memory card when this is lit or blinking.

19. Multi-Function Lock Switch: When engaged, it locks the Main Dial, Quick Command Dial, and Multi-Controller so they cannot change settings.

20. Ambient Light Sensor: Used to measure the ambient light and automatically adjust the LCD monitor's brightness.

21. Speaker: Used to play sound.

22. LCD Monitor: Shows menus, image review, and movie/live-view shooting.

23. Erase Button: Press to erase the currently displayed image. Use the Quick Control Dial to select Cancel or Erase, then press SET.

24. Playback Button: Displays the last photo taken. Use the Quick Control Dial to scroll through the images on the memory card. Press this button again or press the Shutter Release button to exit playback.

25. Index/Magnify/Reduce Button: Zooms out to index view/Zooms in/Zooms out to full screen during playback.

26. RATE Button: Used to assign a rating to images during playback mode.

27. Creative Photo/Direct Print/Comparative Playback Button: In shooting mode, this button opens access to Pictures Styles, Multiple Exposures, and HDR modes. (In Live View, only Picture Styles is available.)/In playback mode, this button allows for direct printing when the camera is attached to a PictBridge-compatible device./ In playback mode, opens the Comparative Photo display.

28. MENU Button: Opens and closes the menu screens on the LCD monitor. When in a submenu, pressing the MENU button returns you to the main menu.

29. INFO Button: In shooting mode, press this button to cycle through the Electronic Level, Camera Settings, and Shooting Functions screens. When in the Shooting Functions screen, you can access and change the shutter speed, aperture, ISO, battery status, and image quality settings. When in Live View or Movie mode, press this button to cycle through four screens: basic information, full information, full information with live histogram, and a clean uncluttered screen showing the active focus area. In playback mode, press this button to cycle through three views of the image: a single frame of the image, a view with basic information, and a detailed view with a thumbnail and brightness histogram.

CAMERA BODY FRONT

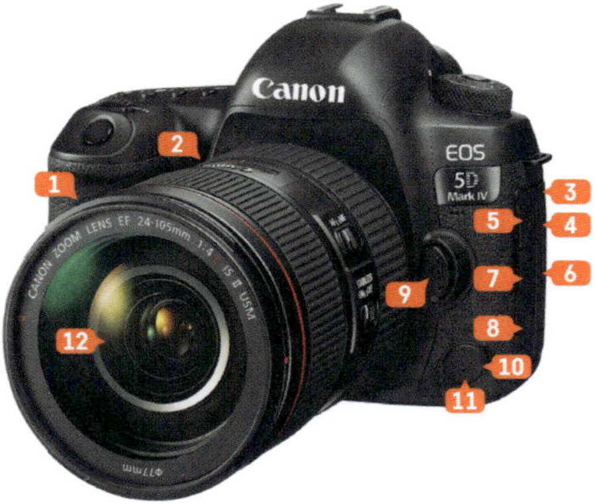

1. **Remote Control Sensor:** Infrared sensor that detects Canon remotes.
2. **Self-Timer Lamp:** Flashes when you are using the self-timer drive mode.
3. **PC Terminal (Under Cover):** Use to connect a sync cable to the camera.
4. **HDMI Out (Under Cover):** Use to connect the camera to a HDMI-compatible display device.
5. **Microphone In (Under Cover):** Use to connect an external microphone.
6. **Digital Terminal (Under Cover):** Use a data transfer cable to connect the camera to a computer.
7. **Headphone Terminal (Under Cover):** Use as an audio out. This is especially useful to monitor audio when recording movies.

8. **Cable Protector Socket (Under Cover):** Use when connecting an interface cable to keep the cable from inadvertently becoming detached.

9. **Lens Release Button:** Press and hold this button to unlock the lens so it can be rotated and removed.

10. **Terminal Cover:** Cover for the remote control port.

11. **Remote Control Terminal (Under Cover):** A three-pin port used to connect a variety of devices to the camera.

12. **Depth of Field Preview Button (Other Side of Lens):** When pressed, the viewfinder shows you what will be in focus with the current aperture. The view will darken as you use smaller apertures.

CAMERA BODY BOTTOM

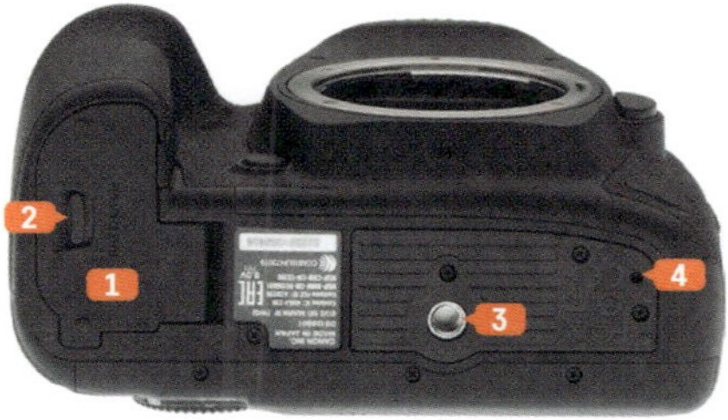

1. **Battery Compartment:** Houses the battery.
2. **Battery Compartment Cover Release:** Use to open the battery compartment.
3. **Tripod Socket:** Standard threaded hole to attach tripods, monopods, and other accessories.
4. **Accessory Positioning Hole:** Use this to make sure you are positioning a battery grip (optional) correctly.

VIEWFINDER

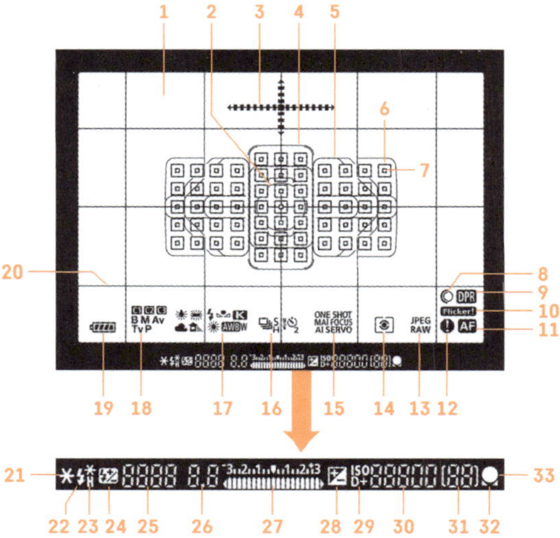

1. **Focusing Screen:** Shows you the scene you are shooting.
2. **Spot Metering Circle:** Area used for spot metering.
3. **Electronic Level:** Shows whether the camera body is level.
4. **Large Zone AF Frame:** Shows the area used for Large Zone Auto Focus.
5. **Area AF Frame:** Group of focus points used together to focus.
6. **Single AF Point:** The single square area used for focusing.
7. **Spot AF Point:** The smallest focusing area—the spot inside the single AF point.

8. **Digital Lens Optimizer:** Shows when the Digital Lens Optimizer (lens correcting database) is enabled.
9. **Dual Pixel RAW Shooting:** Shows when dual pixel raw shooting is on.
10. **Flicker Detection:** Shows when Anti-Flicker Shoot (Shooting [Screen 4]) is enabled.
11. **AF Status Indicator:** Shows the AF mode that is currently active.
12. **Warning:** Illuminates when any of the following conditions are met: the picture style is set to Monochrome; the white balance correction is set; the image recording quality has been changed with the one-touch image-setting function; the High ISO Noise Reduction is set to Multi Shot Noise Reduction; or HDR mode is active.
13. **JPEG/RAW:** Shows if you are saving files as JPEG, RAW, or both.
14. **Metering Mode:** Shows the current metering mode.
15. **AF Operation:** Shows the current AF operation mode.
16. **Drive Mode:** Shows the current drive mode.
17. **White Balance:** Shows the current white balance.
18. **Shooting Mode:** Shows the current shooting mode.
19. **Battery Level:** Shows the current battery life.
20. **Grid:** Helpful for composition and keeping lines in your image straight.
21. **AE Lock/AEB In-Progress:** Shows when auto exposure is locked/ Shows when auto exposure bracketing is active.
22. **Flash Ready/Improper FE Lock Warning:** Shows when the flash is ready to fire/Shows when the flash exposure lock has been applied for an improper amount.
23. **FE Lock/FEB in progress/High-Speed Sync:** Shows when flash exposure is locked/Shows when flash exposure bracketing is active/ Shows when high-speed sync is active.
24. **Flash Exposure Compensation:** Shows when flash exposure compensation is applied.

25. Shutter Speed/Bulb/FE Lock/Busy/Multi Function Lock Warning/No Card Warning/Error Code/AF Point Selection/AF Point Registration/Card Capacity Warning/Card Full Warning: Shows the current shutter speed/Shows when Bulb mode (buLB) is active/Shows when flash exposure lock (FEL) is active/Shows when camera is busy (BuSY)/Shows when the multi function lock warning (L) is active/ Shows when there is no memory card in the camera (Card)/Shows when there is an error code (Err)/Shows when the AF point is being selected ([ ] AF, SEL [], SEL AF)/Shows the auto focus point registration ([ ] HP, SEL [], SEL HP)/Shows a warning when the memory card is nearly full (Card 1/2/1,2)/Shows when the memory card is full (FuLL 1/2/1,2).

26. Aperture/Dust Delete Data Acquisition: Shows current aperture/ Shows when doing the dust delete data acquisition.

27. Exposure Level Indicator/Exposure Compensation Amount/AEB Range/Flash Exposure Compensation: Shows the current exposure level/Shows the exposure compensation amount/Shows the auto exposure bracketing amount/Shows any flash exposure compensation.

28. Exposure Compensation: Shows when exposure compensation is applied.

29. Highlight Tone Priority: Shows when highlight tone priority is enabled.

30. ISO: Shows the current ISO.

31. Maximum Burst/Number of Remaining Multiple Exposures: Shows the number of frames that can be taken in continuous shooting/ Shows the number of frames left when shooting multiple exposures.

32. AF Status Indicator: Shows when the camera is actively focusing.

33. Focus Indicator: Illuminates when the camera believes focus has been achieved.

LCD PANEL

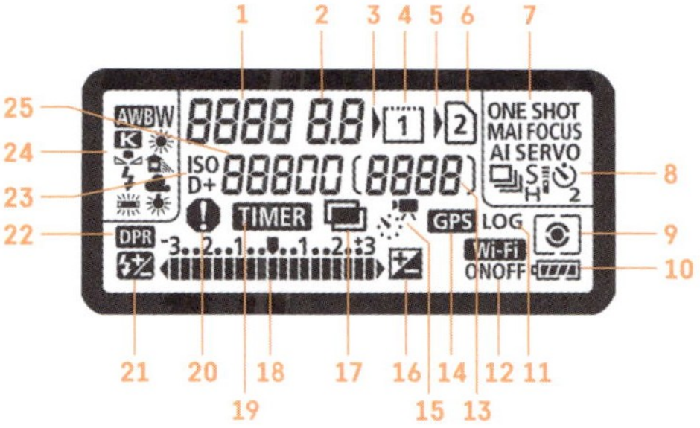

1. Shutter Speed/Bulb/FE Lock/Remaining Number of Exposures for Time-Lapse Movie/Busy/Multi Function Lock Warning/Cleaning the Image Sensor/No Card Warning/Error Code/AF Point Selection/ AF Point Registration/Card Capacity Warning/Card Full Warning: Shows the current shutter speed/Shows when Bulb mode (buLb) is active/Shows when flash exposure lock (FEL) is active/Shows the number of exposures remaining to be taken to create a time-lapse movie/Shows when the camera is busy (buSY)/Shows when the multi function lock warning (L) is active/Shows when the camera is cleaning the image sensor (CLn)/Shows when there is no memory card in the camera (Card)/Shows when there is an error code (Err)/Shows when the AF point is being selected ([ ] AF, SEL [], SEL AF)/Shows the auto focus point registration ([ ] HP, SEL [], SEL HP)/Shows a warning when the memory card is nearly full (Card 1/2/1,2)/Shows when the memory card is full (FuLL 1/2/1,2).

2. Aperture/Dust Delete Data Acquisition: Shows the current aperture/ Shows when doing the dust delete data acquisition.

3. CF Card Selection Icon: Shows when the CF memory card is selected.

4. CF Card Indicator: Shows that there is a CF memory card in the camera.

5. SD Card Selection Icon: Shows when the SD memory card is selected.

6. SD Card Indicator: Shows that there is a SD memory card in the camera.

7. AF Operation: Shows the current AF operation mode.

8. Drive Mode: Shows the current drive mode.

9. Metering Mode: Shows the current metering mode.

10. Battery Level: Shows the current battery life.

11. Logging: Shows when the GPS logging function is active.

12. Wi-Fi Function: Shows when Wi-Fi is on or off.

13. Possible Shots/Self Timer Countdown/Bulb Exposure Time/ Card Error Warning/Error Number/Remaining Images to Record: Shows the possible shots available/Counts down during self-timer mode/Shows the exposure time when shooting in Bulb mode/Shows when there is a memory card error/Shows the number of remaining images left to record.

14. GPS Acquisition Status: Show when GPS is active.

15. Time Lapse Movie Shooting: Shows when time-lapse movie shooting is active.

16. Exposure Compensation: Shows when exposure compensation is active.

17. Multiple Exposure: Shows when you're shooting multiple exposures.

18. Exposure Level Indicator/Exposure Compensation Amount/AEB Range/Flash Exposure Compensation Amount: Shows the exposure level/Shows the exposure compensation amount/Shows the auto exposure bracketing range/Shows the flash exposure compensation amount.

19. Bulb Timer Shooting/Interval Timer Shooting: Shows when Bulb shooting or interval timer shooting is active.

20. Warning: Illuminates when any of the following conditions are met: the picture style is set to Monochrome; the white balance correction is set; the image recording quality has been changed with the one-touch image-setting function; the High ISO Noise Reduction is set to Multi Shot Noise Reduction; or HDR mode is active.

21. Flash Exposure Compensation: Shows when flash exposure compensation is applied.

22. Dual Pixel Raw Shooting: Shows when dual pixel raw shooting is on.

23. Highlight Tone Priority: Shows when the highlight tone priority setting is active.

24. White Balance: Shows the current white balance.

25. ISO: Shows the current ISO.

03 ESSENTIAL MODES AND SETTINGS

SHOOTING MODE

Press the Mode Dial Lock Release down, and turn the Mode Dial to the desired shooting mode.

A+ (Scene Intelligent Auto): This is a fully automatic mode. The camera assesses the scene and determines the optimum settings automatically. It will even adjust the focus on both still and moving subjects, picking the subject closest to the camera.

P (Program Auto Exposure): The camera sets the shutter speed and the aperture based on metering info and the current ISO.

Tv (Time Value, or Shutter Priority Auto Exposure): You set the shutter speed, and the camera sets the aperture based on metering info and the current ISO.

Av (Aperture Value, or Aperture Priority Auto Exposure): You set the aperture, and the camera sets the shutter speed based on metering info and the current ISO. The range of available apertures depends on the attached lens.

M (Manual Exposure): You set the ISO, shutter speed, and aperture. Refer to the exposure level indicator.

B (Bulb): Used for long exposures. The shutter stays open as long as you hold down the Shutter Release button. Use the Main Dial to set the aperture.

C1, C2, C3 (Custom Shooting Modes): You can set up three custom shooting presets here. Use the Set-Up (Screen 4) menu.

METERING MODE

Press the White Balance/Metering Mode button, then turn the Main Dial to select a metering mode.

Evaluative: General-purpose mode suited for most situations and subjects (even backlit subjects).

Partial: Uses 6.1% of the area at the center of the viewfinder for determining the exposure. This is a good choice when there is very bright light around the subject.

Spot: Uses 1.3% of the area at the center of the viewfinder. Use when you need to meter on a specific part of the scene.

Center-Weighted Average: The camera analyzes the whole scene to determine the exposure, but it places more emphasis on the information at the center of the viewfinder.

[Q] QUICK CONTROL

Press the Quick Control button to open the Quick Control screen, where you can set the following: AF method, AF operation, drive mode, metering mode, recording/playing back card and image quality, white balance, picture style, and Auto Lighting Optimizer.

Note: When taking still images, Quick Control works for all the shooting modes; however, when you use Scene Intelligent Auto mode, the following options are not available: AF operation, metering mode, white balance, picture style, and Auto Lighting Optimizer.

[+/–] EXPOSURE COMPENSATION

Press the Shutter Release button halfway down, then rotate the Quick Control Dial to adjust the exposure compensation. You can adjust from –3 (darker) to +3 (lighter) stops, in 1/3-stop increments in the P, Tv, and Av shooting modes.

Note: You can actually set the exposure compensation from –5 to +5 stops by using the Quick Control feature (see above). The LCD panel shows only +/–3 stops.

Note: The exposure compensation you set will remain in effect until you change it. It does not reset to 0 when the camera is turned off.

FOCUS OPERATION

Press the Drive/AF button, then select the AF operation mode using the Main Dial.

One-Shot AF: Focus starts when the Shutter Release button is pressed halfway, then locks when focus is achieved. Best for stationary subjects.

AI Servo AF: Focus starts when the Shutter Release button is pressed halfway and continues to focus until the photo is taken. Best for moving subjects.

AI Focus AF: This mode automatically switches between the One-Shot AF and the AI Servo AF modes depending on the subject. The camera focuses on the subject and locks focus when the subject stops moving (One-Shot AF), but if it senses the subject moving again, it will switch to AI Servo AF and start focusing again.

Note: For Manual focus, set the AF/MF switch on the lens to MF, and rotate the focus ring on the lens barrel to focus.

AUTOFOCUS (AF) AREA AND POINT SELECTION

Press the AF Point Selection button, then cycle through the AF area selection modes by pressing the AF Area Selection button.

Single-Point Spot AF: The smallest focusing area. Used for pinpoint focusing.

Single-Point AF: Uses a single focusing square.

AF Point Expansion: The camera uses the selected AF point and the four adjacent AF points to achieve focus.

AF Point Expansion, Surrounding Points: The camera uses the selected AF point and the eight surrounding AF points to achieve focus.

Zone AF: One of nine focusing zones is used to achieve focus.

Large Zone AF: One of three focusing zones (left, center, or right) is used to achieve focus.

Automatic Selection AF: The entire AF area frame is used to achieve focus.

Move the AF point or Zone AF frame: Press the AF Point button, then use the Multi-Controller to move the selected AF point or zone. You can also rotate the Main Dial to move the AF point horizontally or the Quick Control Dial to move the AF point vertically.

Note: The camera has 61 AF points, but the number of usable focus points depends on the lens attached to the camera.

DRIVE MODE

Press the Drive/AF Button, then rotate the Quick Control Dial to select the desired drive mode.

Single Shooting: The camera takes a single shot every time you press the Shutter Release button.

High-Speed Continuous Shooting: The camera takes up to 7 frames per second (FPS) when you press and hold the Shutter Release button. This FPS rate slows down under the following conditions:

- **Anti-Flicker Shooting:** Continuous shooting speed is 6.6 FPS.
- **Dual Pixel Raw Shooting:** Continuous shooting speed is 5 FPS.
- **Live View Shooting:** When AF operation is set to One-Shot AF and Silent Live View shooting is disabled, the continuous shooting speed is 7 FPS. When AF operation is set to Servo AF, the continuous shooting speed is 4.3 FPS.
- **Digital Lens Optimizer:** When this is enabled, the continuous shooting speed is greatly reduced.

Low-Speed Continuous Shooting: The camera takes up to 3 frames per second when you press and hold the Shutter Release button.

Silent Single Shooting: The camera takes a single frame every time the Shutter Release button is pressed; the mechanical shutter sound is also reduced. Cannot be used during Live View shooting.

Silent Continuous Shooting: The camera takes up to 3 frames per second when you press and hold the Shutter Release button; the mechanical shutter sound is also reduced. Cannot be used during Live View shooting.

Self-Timer 10: Sets the self-timer for 10 seconds before taking the shot.

Self-Timer 2: Sets the self-timer for 2 seconds before taking the shot.

WHITE BALANCE

Press the White Balance/Metering button and rotate the Quick Control Dial to select the white balance.

Auto (AWB) setting is best for most situations. AWB-W (Auto–White Priority) is best when you want to reduce a warm color cast. White balance settings reflect different lighting conditions. Match the white balance to the type of lighting you're in to render the scene with the truest colors. The available settings are Daylight, Shade, Cloudy/Twilight/Sunset, Tungsten, White Fluorescent, Flash, Custom, and Color Temperature.

FILE FORMAT

MENU > Shooting (Screen 1) > Image Quality. Use the Main Dial to select the RAW quality, and use the Quick Control Dial to select the JPEG quality.

RAW: The RAW data from the image sensor is recorded each time a photo is taken. There are three RAW image quality settings: RAW (full size), M RAW (medium), and S RAW (small).

JPEG: The camera saves a JPEG file each time the Shutter Release button is pressed. You can choose from among eight sizes of JPEG.

RAW/JPEG: If you have selected a RAW and a JPEG option, the camera saves two files each time the Shutter Release button is pressed: a RAW file and a JPEG file. You decide the sizes of the RAW and JPEG files.

04 OTHER HELPFUL SETTINGS

PICTURE STYLE

Press the Creative Photo button, select the picture style icon, then select the picture style you would like to use. Eight preset picture styles can be selected to apply to JPEG images: **A (Auto), S (Standard), P (Portrait), L (Landscape), FD (Fine Detail), N (Neutral), F (Faithful), M (Monochrome)**. The Monochrome setting has four color filters: Yellow, Orange, Red, and Green. You can customize each picture style by adjusting the Sharpness (Strength, Fineness, and Threshold), Contrast, Saturation, Color Tone, Filter Effect (Monochrome), and Toning Effect (Monochrome). Finally, there are three user-defined picture styles available, which allow you to customize and save any of the styles for easy access later.

CUSTOM WHITE BALANCE

Setting a custom white balance can help you get the best color when you're shooting under mixed lighting:

1. Take a photo of a white card (or a white wall) under the mixed lighting of the scene.
2. Select MENU > Shooting (Screen 2) > Custom White Balance, and press SET.
3. The last photo taken will be shown (if not, use the Quick Control Dial to navigate to it), and press SET.

COLOR SPACE

MENU > Shooting (Screen 2) > Color Space

sRGB: Smaller color space. Best when images are used directly from the camera.

Adobe RGB: Larger color space. Best used when images will be edited with post-processing software later.

DUAL PIXEL RAW

MENU > Shooting (Screen 1) Dual Pixel RAW

This is a special RAW format that saves two copies of the RAW file, allowing for micro adjustments of the image during post-processing. This can help increase the sharpness, adjust

bokeh in the out-of-focus areas, and reduce ghosting. It does take up twice as much space on your memory cards, and it requires more post-processing. You must also use Canon's Digital Photo Professional software. To use Dual Pixel RAW shooting, you must be shooting full-sized RAW files, and it works best with a focal length of 50mm or greater, an ISO of 1600 or lower, and an aperture of f/5.6 or lower.

HIGHLIGHT ALERT (BLINKIES)

MENU > Playback (Screen 3) > Highlight Alert

Select Enable so that clipped highlights will blink, indicating possible overexposure in your images. To obtain more detail in those areas, adjust the exposure settings or exposure compensation, and shoot again.

HIGHLIGHT TONE PRIORITY

MENU > Shooting (Screen 3) > Highlight Tone Priority

Select Enable to improve the rendering of details in highlights of the images you shoot. When shooting with this setting enabled, the lowest ISO you can use is 200, and you cannot use expanded ISO speeds.

NOISE REDUCTION

MENU > Shooting (Screen 3) > Long Exposure Noise Reduction

Reduces noise in images with shutter speeds of 1 second or longer. Using this feature doubles the time it takes to save the image to the memory card. Choices are Auto, Enable, and Disable. Auto is usually the best choice.

MENU > Shooting (Screen 3) > High ISO Speed Noise Reduction

Reduces noise in images taken at high ISO settings. Use Standard for default, Low for less noise reduction, and High for more noise reduction. Only affects JPEG images.

AUTO ISO

MENU > Shooting (Screen 2) > ISO Speed Settings

Within the ISO Speed Settings, select Auto for the ISO Speed, then use the Auto Range option to set the minimum and maximum ISO settings to define the range that the camera can use. You can also set the Minimum Shutter Speed to ensure that the camera does not lower the shutter speed too much; this helps reduce camera shake and blurry images.

EXPOSURE BRACKETING

You can bracket a set of three exposures up to +/–3 stops in 1/3-stop increments:

1. Select MENU > Shooting (Screen 2) > Exposure Compensation/AEB.

2. Set the Bracketing range by turning the Main Dial.

3. If desired, set the exposure compensation amount by turning the Quick Control Dial. Press SET.

4. Take the pictures, and three bracketed shots will be created. (If you're in Single shooting drive mode, take three pictures to create the bracketed sequence. If you're in a Continuous shooting drive mode, the three shots will be taken together when you press and hold the Shutter Release button.)

Note: Bracketing will remain on until you set the bracketing range back to 0.

WIRELESS CONNECTION

Install the Camera Connect app on your smartphone and pair it with the Canon 5D Mark IV.

This will allow you to view and transfer images to your smartphone, see the Live View image on your smartphone, and even shoot remotely from your smartphone.

RESET CAMERA

MENU > Set-Up (Screen 5) > Clear All Camera Settings

Resets all camera settings for shooting functions and menu functions to their factory defaults.

05 STEP-BY-STEP SHOOTING INSTRUCTIONS

MULTIPLE EXPOSURES

Create in-camera multiple exposures, where you can shoot 2–9 images that are then merged into a single JPEG image:

1. Press the Creative Photo button, select the icon for multiple exposures, and press SET. (You can also select MENU > Shooting [Screen 3] > Multiple Exposure.)
2. Choose a shooting option:

   On: Function/Control: Choose this if you want to shoot gradually and check the results as you shoot.

   On: Continuous Shooting: Choose this if you want to shoot continuous multiple exposures of moving subjects.
3. Choose a Multiple Exposure Control option:

   Additive: The exposure of each image is added cumulatively.

   Average: Based on the number of exposures you set (Step 4), negative exposure compensation is added automatically as you shoot to achieve a standard overall exposure.

   Bright: Retains brightest portion of the images you shoot.

   Dark: Retains darkest portion of the images you shoot.

4. Set the Number of Exposures you'd like to combine. You can combine 2–9 exposures.
5. Specify whether you'd like to save all the individual images (All Images) or just the resulting multiple exposure (Result Only).
6. Set a Continue Multiple Exposure option:
   1-Shot Only: Shoot just one multiple exposure.
   Continuously: Continue shooting multiple exposures until you disable the feature.
7. Shoot all of the exposures and they will be combined into one multiple exposure.

Note: When shooting using the Function/Control method (Step 1), you can press the Erase button after taking individual shots; this lets you recapture a shot, exit the multiple exposure, etc.

HDR HDR

Combine three images to reduce the contrast and improve tonal range. The camera generates one JPEG image as the resulting HDR image:

1. Press the Creative Photo button, select the icon for HDR, and press SET. (You can also select MENU > Shooting [Screen 3] > HDR Mode.)

2. Choose the dynamic range you want:

   Auto: Sets the dynamic range automatically depending on the scene's tonal range.

   +/–1, +/–2, or +/–3: The higher the number, the wider the dynamic range of the image will be.

3. Set an Effect:

   Natural: Preserves a wide tonal range. Clipped highlights and shadows are reduced.

   Art Standard: The picture will look a bit more like a painting. The clipped highlights and shadows are reduced more than Natural, but the contrast is lower.

   Art Vivid: More saturated colors, and there is a graphic art effect.

   Art Bold: Most saturated colors. The subject pops, and the image looks more like an oil painting.

   Art Embossed: Saturation, brightness, contrast, and gradation are decreased for an overall flat image. Creates a faded and old look.

4. Select an option for Continuous HDR:

   1 Shot Only: Shoot just one HDR image.

   Every Shot: Continue shooting HDR images until you disable HDR shooting.

5. Select the Auto Image Align setting:
   Enable: Choose this if you're shooting handheld.
   Disable: Choose if you're shooting on a tripod.
6. Select an option for Save Source Images: You can save all the images that you shoot (All Images) or just the resulting HDR image (HDR Image Only).
7. Take the picture.

TIME-LAPSE MOVIES

Create a time-lapse movie in-camera:

1. Pick a shooting mode, then set the Live View/Movie switch to the movie icon.
2. Select MENU > Shooting (Screen 5) > Time-Lapse Movie, select Enable, then press the INFO button.
3. Set the Interval and the Number of Shots. Select OK and review the settings.
4. Press the MENU button to exit the menu screen, read the message that appears (about taking a test shot), and select OK. Take some test shots until you're happy with the result.
5. Press the Start/Stop button, then press the Shutter Release button to start shooting the time-lapse movie.

06 TYPICAL SHOOTING SCENARIOS

SHOOTING SCENARIO
PORTRAIT

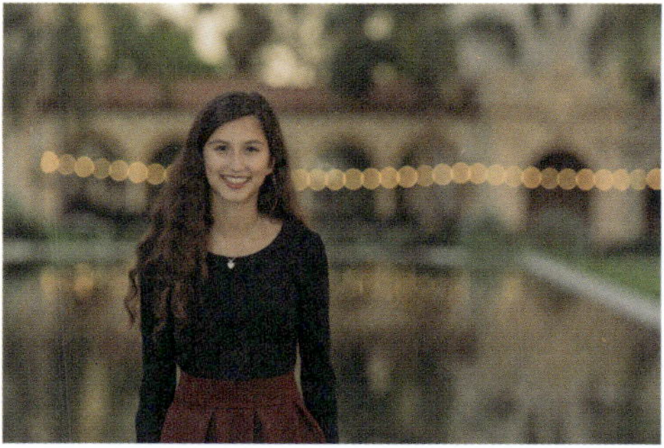

KEY PRINCIPLES

- The key to a portrait like this is shallow depth of field. So shoot in **APERTURE PRIORITY (Av)** mode and start with the lowest aperture your lens offers (such as **f/2.8 or f/4**).
- Remember to **focus on the eyes**.
- If the image is too dark or too light, use **EXPOSURE COMPENSATION** to adjust the brightness level.

- If the image is blurry from a slow shutter speed, **raise the ISO** to increase your sensor's sensitivity to light, thus allowing for a faster shutter speed.
- Remember to use a **focal length of 50mm or greater** so that you don't distort your subject's face.

SHOOTING SCENARIO
GROUP PORTRAIT

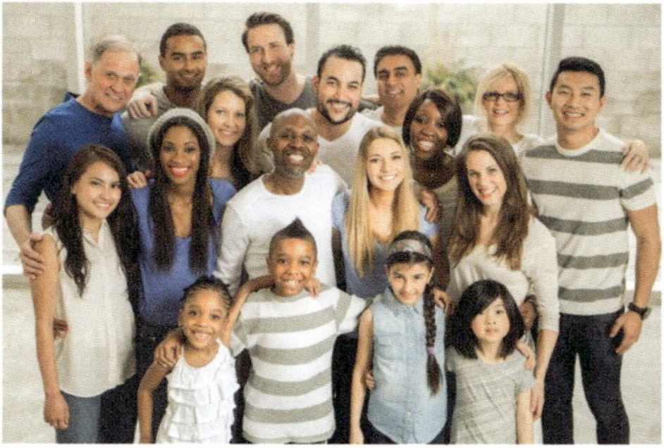

KEY PRINCIPLES

- In order to get everyone in focus, you need a deep depth of field. So shoot in **APERTURE PRIORITY (Av)** mode and set the aperture between **f/8–f/16**.

- **Focus on the person in the middle of the group**. Check the focus by using the LCD screen. View it at 100%, and check the faces in the front and back rows. If anyone is out of focus, use a smaller aperture for deeper depth of field.
- Use **EVALUATIVE METERING** to account for the light in the entire scene.
- **Arrange the group so they can all see you** (and you can see them).
- Use **EXPOSURE COMPENSATION** if the image is too bright or too dark.
- If image is blurry, **raise the ISO** to allow the camera to use a faster shutter speed.

SHOOTING SCENARIO

LANDSCAPE

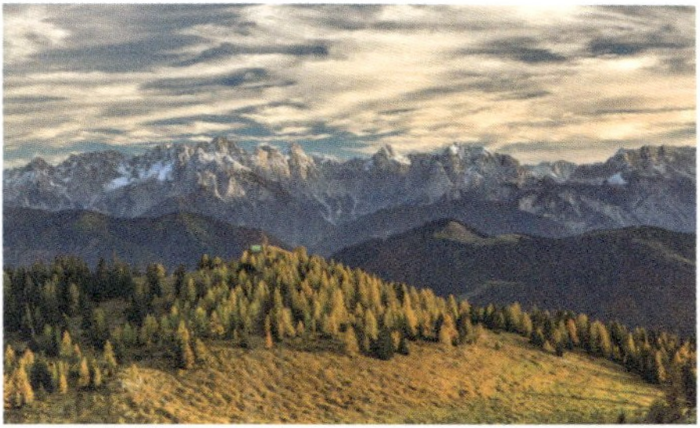

KEY PRINCIPLES

- Shoot in **APERTURE PRIORITY (Av)** mode to control the depth of field, and start with **f/16** to ensure deep depth of field.
- **Use a tripod** to eliminate camera movement. Whenever your camera is on a tripod, also make sure that any **IMAGE STABILIZATION** is turned off.
- Use **EVALUATIVE METERING** and **ONE-SHOT AF** focus operation.
- **Set the ISO to a low setting (100–200)** to avoid any digital noise.
- Shoot in **RAW** so that you have the most available information when editing later.
- Consider **BRACKETING** your exposures.

SHOOTING SCENARIO

FREEZE ACTION

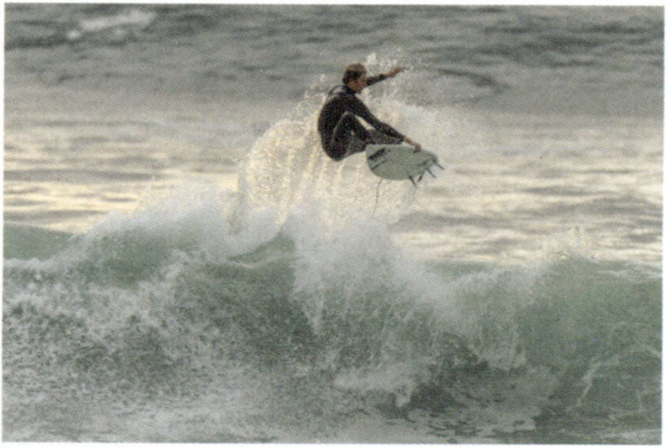

KEY PRINCIPLES

- Use **SHUTTER PRIORITY (Tv)** mode and set the shutter speed to a value that will freeze the action. The appropriate shutter speed depends on your subject and its movement, but could be anywhere from **1/500–1/8000 sec**.
- Use **AI SERVO AF** autofocus operation so that the camera keeps focusing as the subject moves.
- If the image is dark or blurry, **raise the ISO or try AUTO ISO** to automatically have the camera adjust the ISO as needed.

SHOOTING SCENARIO

SHOWING MOTION—PANNING

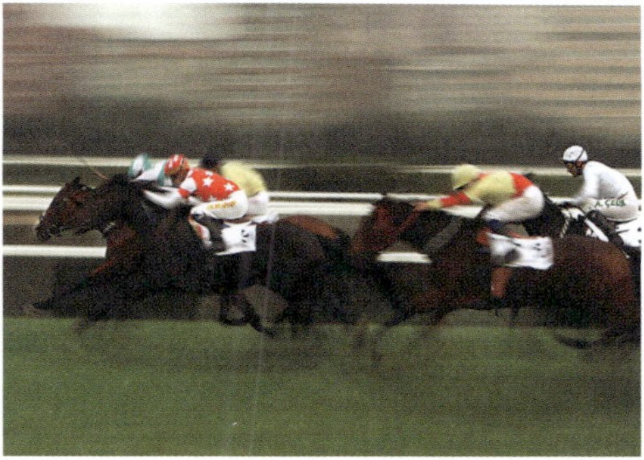

KEY PRINCIPLES

- Shoot in **SHUTTER PRIORITY (Tv)** mode and use a slow-enough shutter speed to allow for the subject to move during the exposure.
- **Follow the subject** across the frame as you shoot.
- Use **AI SERVO AF** autofocus operation, as well as the **AF POINT EXPANSION or ZONE AF** autofocus area, to ensure the camera focuses on the subject.

SHOOTING SCENARIO

LOW-LIGHT ACTION

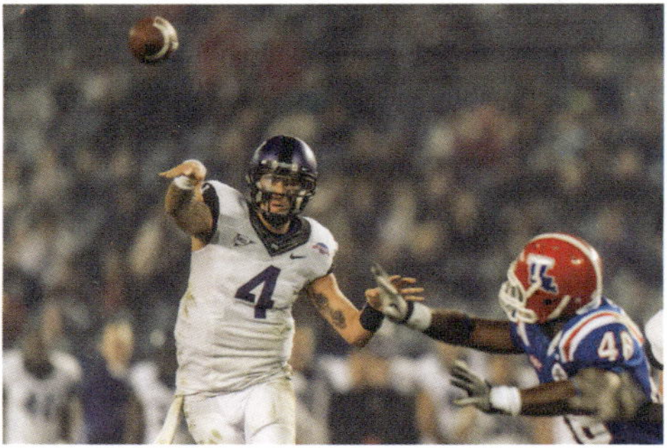

KEY PRINCIPLES

- Shoot in **APERTURE PRIORITY (Av)** mode and use a wide aperture such as **f/2.8 or f/4**.
- Use **PARTIAL METERING** and meter on the subject's face.
- Use **AI SERVO AF** autofocus operation and **SINGLE-POINT AF** (a single focus point).
- **Set the ISO to 1600 or higher**, depending on the amount of available light.
- If the image is blurry, **increase the ISO** to allow for a faster shutter speed.

SHOOTING SCENARIO

LONG EXPOSURE

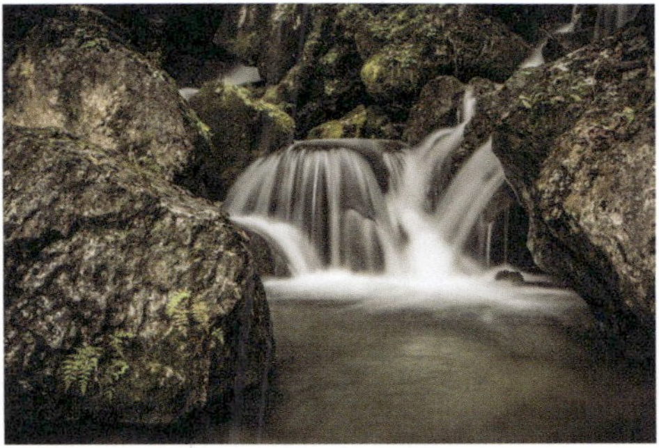

KEY PRINCIPLES

- Use **MANUAL** shooting mode, which allows you to use the **BULB** shutter speed for long exposures.
- **Use a tripod** to keep the camera stable. **Turn off any IMAGE STABILIZATION**.
- Use **ONE-SHOT AF** focus operation, or try manual focus if the camera is having a hard time locking on focus.
- **Use a low ISO (100–400)** and **shoot RAW** to ensure a high-quality file.
- Use a **cable release** with a lock to avoid touching (shaking) the camera.